Your Body

Senses

Anna Sandeman

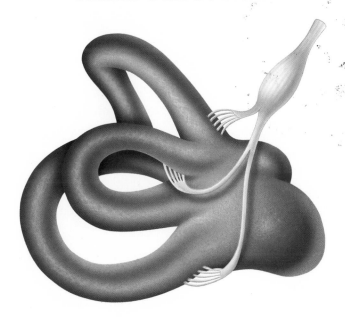

Watts Books
LONDON • SYDNEY

© Aladdin Books Ltd 1995
Designed and produced by
Aladdin Books Ltd
28 Percy Street
London W1P 0LD

First published in Great Britain in 1995 by
Watts Books
96 Leonard Street
London EC2A 4RH

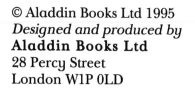

Design: **David West** •
CHILDREN'S BOOK DESIGN
Designer: Edward Simkins
Illustrator: Ian Thompson
Editor: Liz White
Picture Research: Brooks
Krikler Research
Consultants: Dr R Levene MB.BS,
DCH, DRCOG
Jan Bastoncino Dip. Ed., teacher
of biology and science to 5-12
year-olds

ISBN 0-7496-1974-0

Printed in Belgium

A CIP catalogue record for this
book is available from the British
Library.

Photocredits
Abbreviations: t-top, m-middle, b-bottom,
r-right, l-left
All photos in this book are by Roger Vlitos
except: Cover, 6bl, 7mr, 14-15m, 15tl, 15tr,
28tl, & 28-29m Bruce Coleman; 7tl Eye
Ubiquitous; 7br, 26-27t & 29tr Spectrum
Colour Library; 10m Science Photo Library.

Contents

What senses?

All animals, including you, have senses. You have five main senses. You use them to find out about the world around you. Without them, you would not be able to see, hear, smell, taste or touch.

Some animals have fewer senses than you do. They develop those senses which suit their way of life best. Cats and owls, which hunt at night, can see well in the dark.

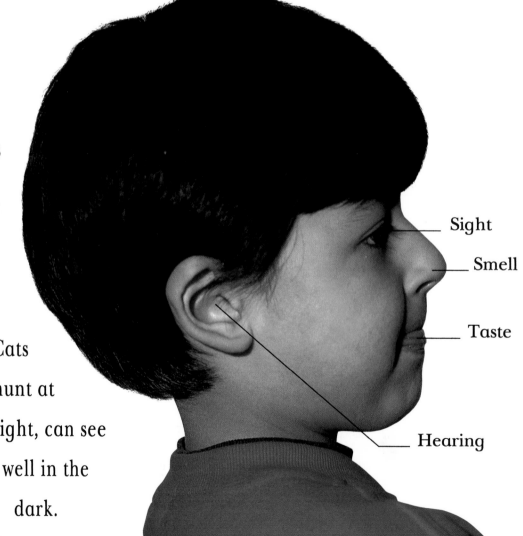

Sight

Smell

Taste

Hearing

It is thought that whales and dolphins can hear each other talking over hundreds of miles of ocean. Dogs, lions and wolves use their keen sense of smell to track down their prey. Snakes use their tongues to collect smells from the air around them. Many insects have well-developed senses to help protect them from other animals.

Touch ———

All animals need their senses to find food and to escape their enemies. We use our senses to keep us safe and to enjoy life.

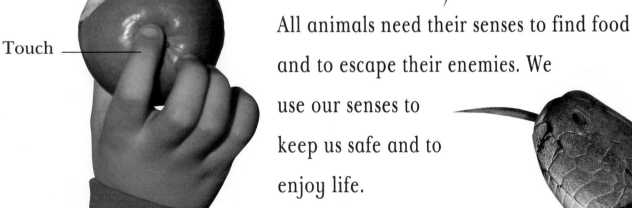

The pupil and the iris

Each of your eyes is like a rubbery ball, about two and a half centimetres across, or the size of a ping-pong ball. In the middle is a black hole called the pupil. Light passes through the pupil to enter your eye.

Around the pupil is a coloured ring of muscles – the iris. Most people have either a brown or blue iris. The iris controls how much light enters the eye. In bright light, the iris makes the pupil smaller to stop too much light getting in. In dim light, it makes the pupil bigger to let in more light.

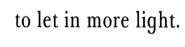

Use a mirror to look at your pupils in a dimly-lit room. Now switch on a light. What happens? Draw what you see.

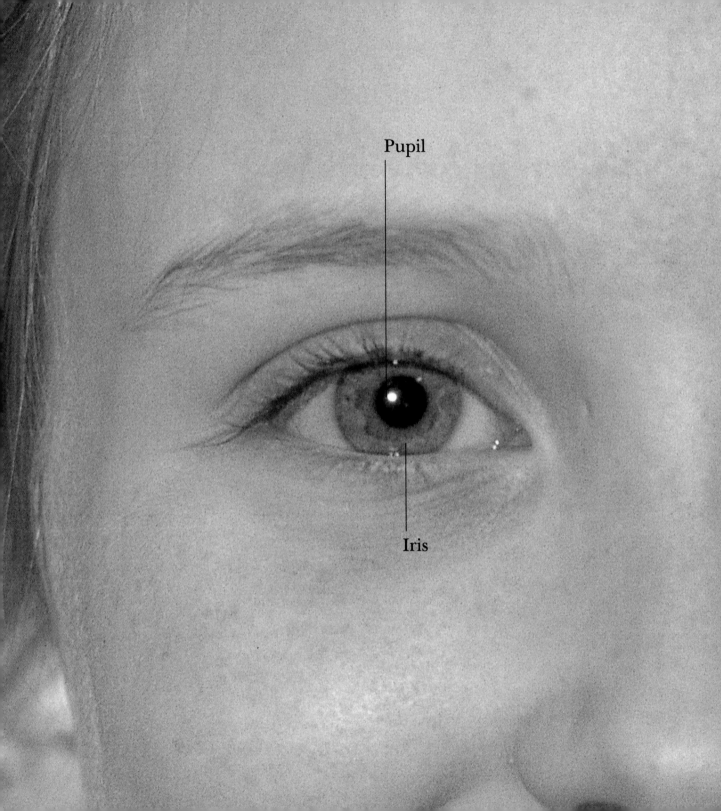

Pupil

Iris

How eyes work

Behind each pupil is a lens. This is like a small, curved piece of jelly. As light enters your eye, the lens bends it to form a tiny upside-down picture of what you see on the retina at the back of your eye.

Your retina is made up of millions of tiny nerve endings. It sends messages along the optic nerve to your brain. The brain sorts out the messages. It turns the picture the right way up, and decides what colour and size everything is.

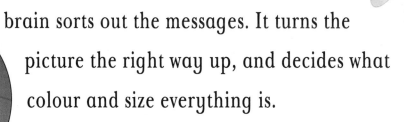

Close-up of the retina, showing blind spot (in yellow)

Part of your retina, your blind spot, is not sensitive to light. Look at the two pictures below. Cover your left eye and look at the apple. Slowly move the book towards you. When the carrot vanishes you have found your blind spot.

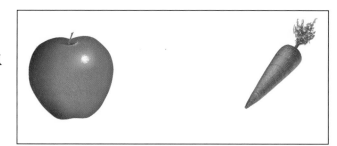

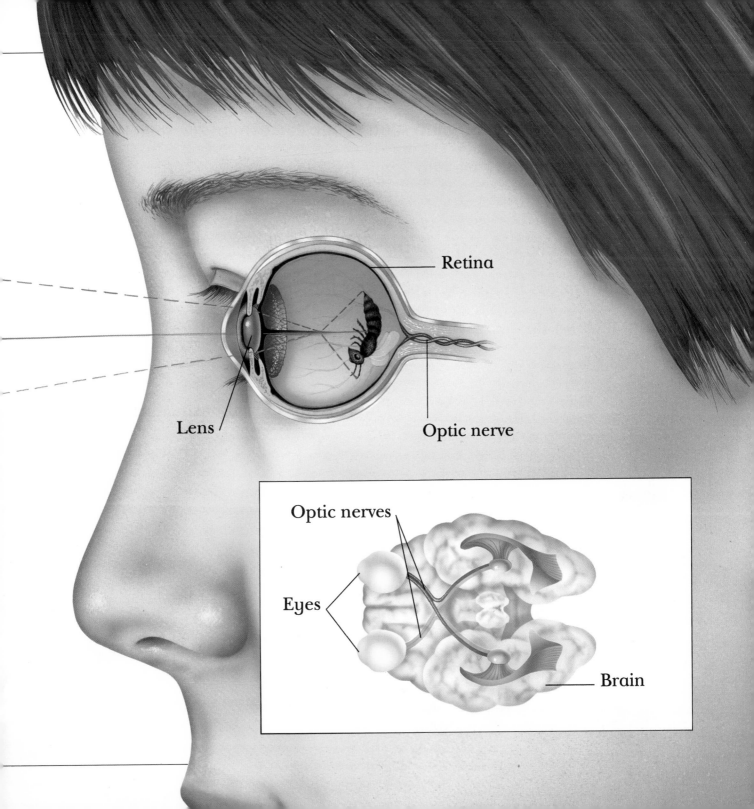

Retina

Lens

Optic nerve

Optic nerves

Eyes

Brain

Working together
Normally you do not notice your blind spot. If one eye cannot see something, the other usually can.

Hold up a pen and close your left eye. Line up the pen with a clock on the wall for example. Now open your left eye and close your right without moving the pen. What happens?

The pen has moved because each of your eyes sees it from a different angle.

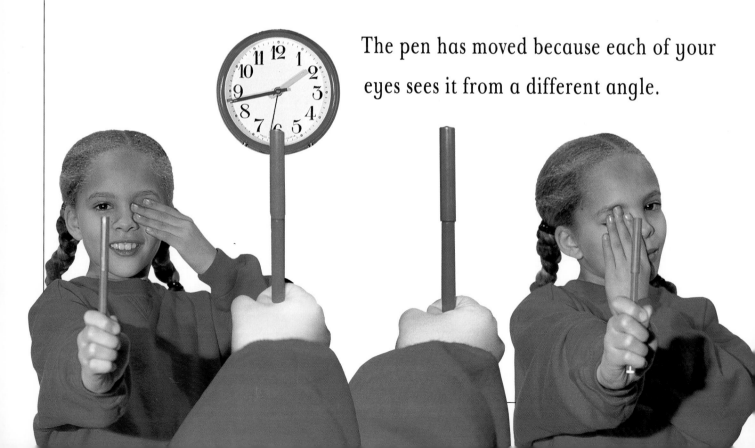

Eye problems

Many people are short-sighted or long-sighted. This means that the picture formed at the back of their eye falls just in front of the retina, or just behind it. Spectacles or contact lenses help them to see clearly.

Long sight

Short sight

A few people are colour blind. This usually means that they cannot tell red from green. Look at this circle of dots. Can you see a number in it?

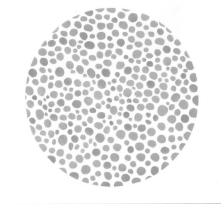

Sound waves

Listen carefully. What sounds can you hear? Are they loud or soft? High or low?

Fill a large bowl with water. Let drops of water fall into the middle of the bowl. Watch the ripples. Sound makes ripples like these in the air. These ripples are called sound waves.

Loud sound

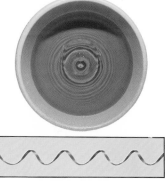

Soft sound

The pitch of a sound – how high or low it is – depends on how many times it vibrates (shakes) each second. The more vibrations, the higher the pitch. Compare the pattern of a mouse's squeak with a lion's roar. Which has more vibrations?

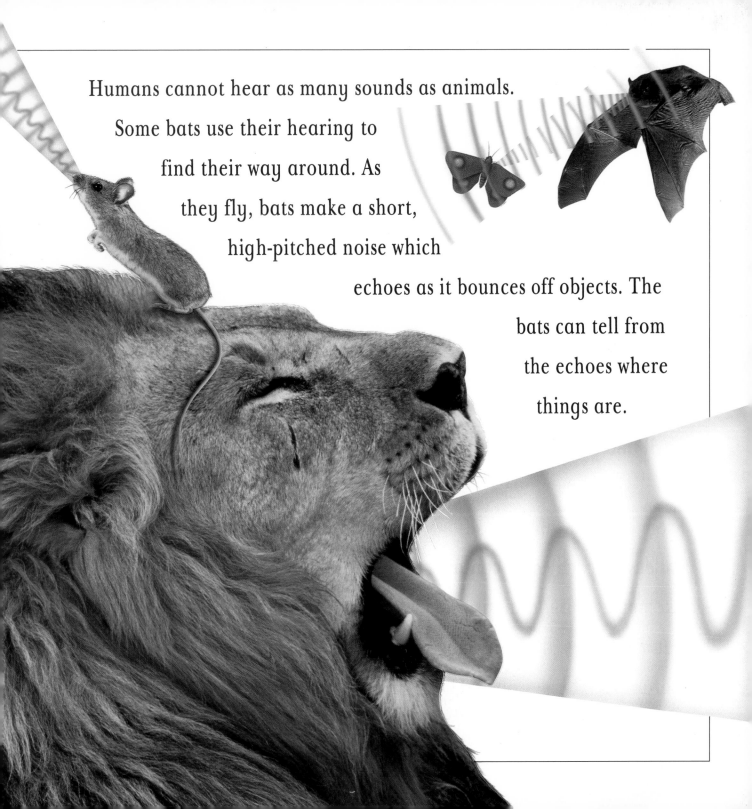

Humans cannot hear as many sounds as animals. Some bats use their hearing to find their way around. As they fly, bats make a short, high-pitched noise which echoes as it bounces off objects. The bats can tell from the echoes where things are.

How ears work

Your ears – the parts you can see – funnel sound waves into your ear canals and on to your eardrums.

Your eardrum is a thin piece of skin stretched across the end of your ear canal. When sound waves touch your eardrum, it vibrates. The vibrations pass from your eardrum to three small bones, the hammer, anvil and stirrup.

From here the vibrations flow to a coiled tube called the cochlea. It contains thousands of hair-like nerve endings and is filled with liquid. When the liquid vibrates, the hairs move and change the vibrations into messages. These messages are sent to your brain, which decides what they mean.

Wax duct

Ear canal

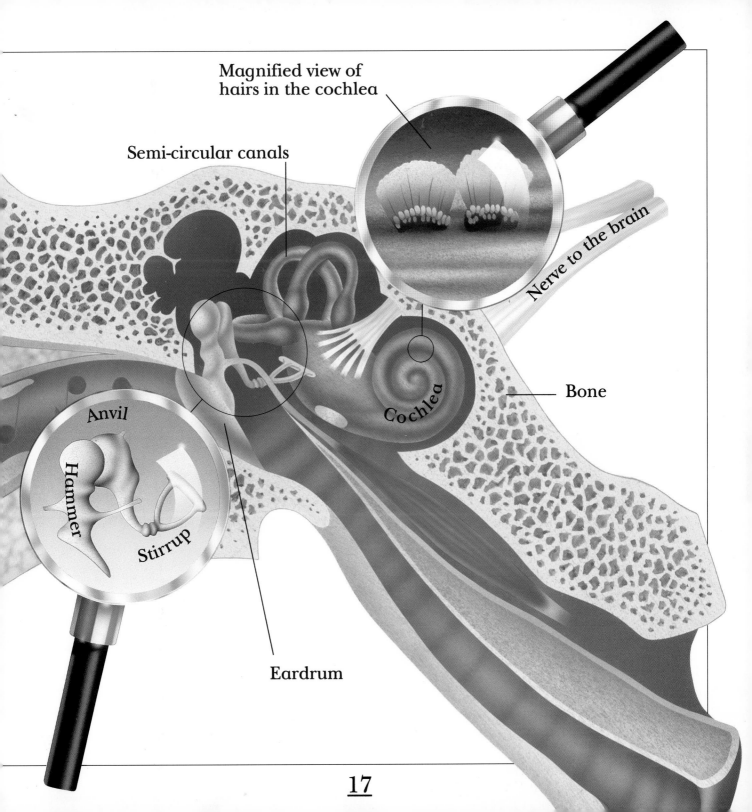

Magnified view of
hairs in the cochlea

Semi-circular canals

Nerve to the brain

Bone

Cochlea

Anvil

Hammer

Stirrup

Eardrum

17

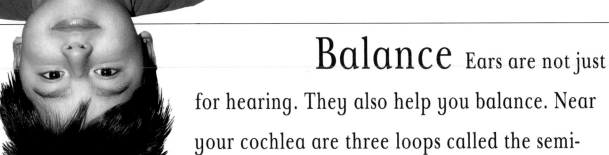

Balance

Ears are not just for hearing. They also help you balance. Near your cochlea are three loops called the semi-circular canals. The canals are full of liquid. When you move your head, the liquid also moves. It pushes against hair-like nerve endings, which send messages to your brain. From these messages your brain can work out what position your head is in.

Semi-circular canal

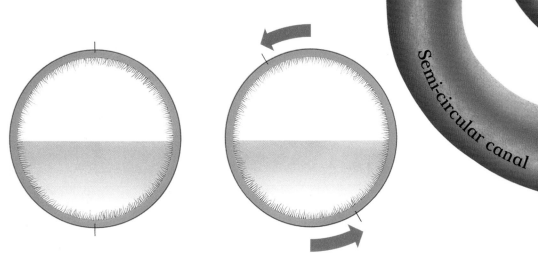

Liquid in the canals moves as you move your head.

Pour a few centimetres of water into a glass jar. Move the jar quickly round so that the water swirls up the sides. Now stop the jar. What happens to the water?

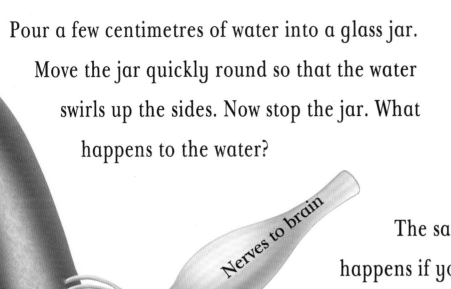

Nerves to brain

The same thing happens if you spin round too fast. When you stop, the liquid in your semi-circular canals keeps moving. The nerve endings go on sending messages to your brain. Meanwhile your eyes tell you that you are standing still. Your brain gets muddled and you feel dizzy.

Smelling

How many smells can you think of? Which do you like? Which do you dislike? Believe it or not, your brain can pick out over 10,000 different smells!

When you breathe in, air travels up your nose and into a space called the nasal cavity. The cavity roof is packed with millions of tiny hairs. They are rooted in a thick, sticky liquid called mucus – like reeds in a pond. Scent particles in the air mix with the mucus and are taken up by the hairs. Nerve endings in the hairs send messages to your brain, and your brain decides what the scent is.

Some smells make you feel happy, others sad. Some make you feel hungry. Others make you feel sick. Smells can warn you not to eat bad food, or tell you that something is burning.

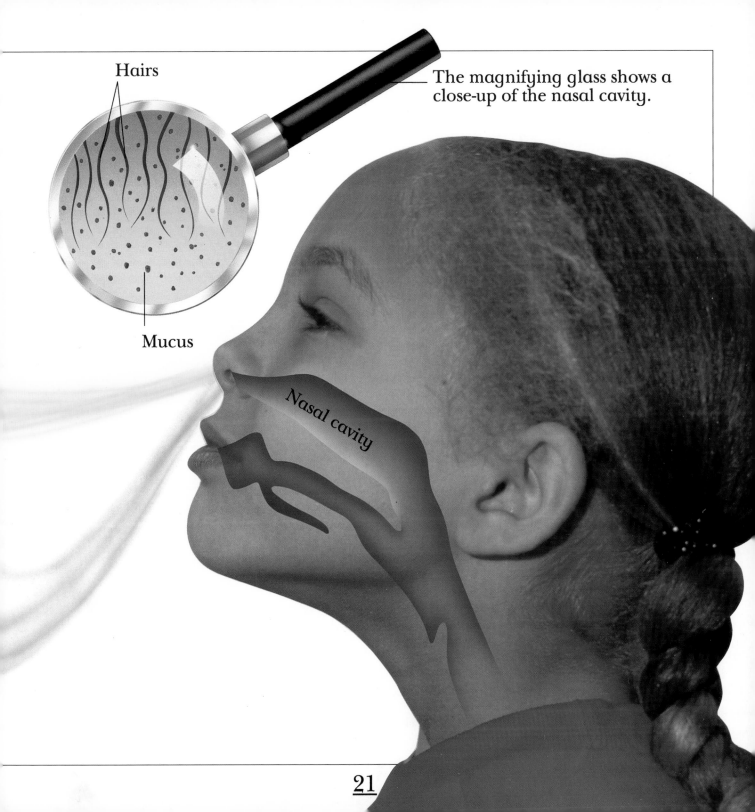

Hairs

Mucus

The magnifying glass shows a close-up of the nasal cavity.

Nasal cavity

Tasting

Look at your tongue in a mirror. Can you see lots of little bumps? Inside each bump there are over a hundred taste buds which pick up different tastes in your food.

You have different taste buds to pick up each type of taste – salt, sweet, sour and bitter. You can find out where they are on your tongue. Use cotton buds to dab in turn salt, sugar, lemon juice (sour) and coffee grounds (bitter) on your tongue. Where does each taste seem strongest?

Close-up of taste buds

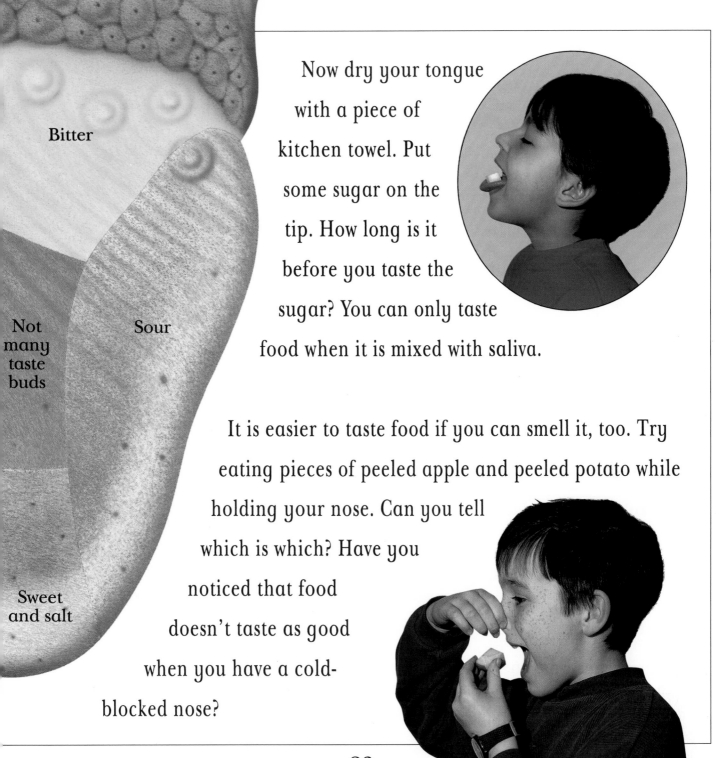

Bitter

Not many taste buds

Sour

Sweet and salt

Now dry your tongue with a piece of kitchen towel. Put some sugar on the tip. How long is it before you taste the sugar? You can only taste food when it is mixed with saliva.

It is easier to taste food if you can smell it, too. Try eating pieces of peeled apple and peeled potato while holding your nose. Can you tell which is which? Have you noticed that food doesn't taste as good when you have a cold-blocked nose?

Touch

The skin that covers your body is full of tiny nerve endings which give you information about things that are in contact with your body.

Shut your eyes and pick fruits from a bowl. Feel each fruit in turn. Can you recognise each one? What makes them different?

Nerve endings in your skin can tell if something is hot or cold, rough or smooth. They can also feel something pressing against you, or hurting you. You have at least 20 types of nerve ending, sending all kinds of messages to your brain.

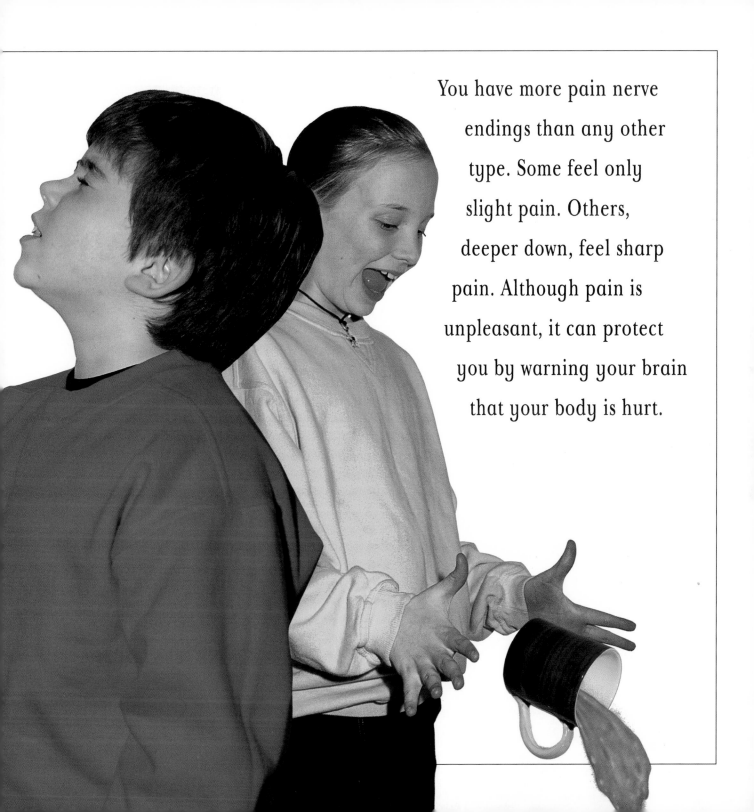

You have more pain nerve endings than any other type. Some feel only slight pain. Others, deeper down, feel sharp pain. Although pain is unpleasant, it can protect you by warning your brain that your body is hurt.

The lighter touch

Some parts of your body have more nerve endings than others. Run a fine paintbrush lightly over your lips. Now along your forearm. Where does it tingle most?

Your fingertips, too, are very sensitive. Blind people use their fingertips to read in Braille, by tracing patterns of raised dots.

If you have ever bitten your tongue you know it can feel pain! But it is less good at sensing heat and cold. Your tongue does not sense quickly enough that something is too hot, so you can easily scald your mouth.

The least sensitive part of your body is the middle of your back. If you have an itch there, it is hard to find the place with a back scratcher. It is easier to get someone else to do it for you!

Did you know?

... that an ostrich has eyes five centimetres across? Each eye weighs more than its brain!

... that a chameleon's eyes can look in opposite directions at the same time?

... that you keep your eyes open almost all the time you are awake? But you do close them to blink. Most people blink every two to ten seconds. How many times do you blink in one minute?

... that each time you blink, you shut your eyes for 0.3 seconds? This means that in one day, your eyes are shut for nearly half an hour.

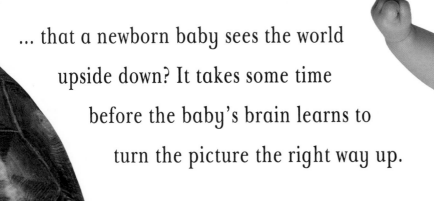

... that a newborn baby sees the world upside down? It takes some time before the baby's brain learns to turn the picture the right way up.

... that a baby has more taste buds than an adult?

... that all tortoises are deaf?

... that children have more sensitive ears than adults? They can recognise a wider variety of pitches.

... that one in every twelve males is colour blind? Colour blindness is much less common in females.

Index

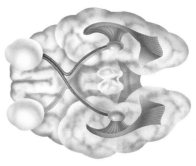